Church Time

The Fellowship of the Three

Exploring the Trinity

Jane Williams

CANTERBURY
PRESS
Norwich

First published in 2006 by the Canterbury Press Norwich
(a publishing imprint of Hymns Ancient &
Modern Limited, a registered charity)
9–17 St Alban's Place, London N1 0NX

www.scm-canterburypress.co.uk

British Library Cataloguing in Publication data

A catalogue record for this book is available
from the British Library

ISBN 1-85311-699-8/978-1-85311-699-5

Typeset by Regent Typesetting, London
Printed and bound by
Gallpen Colour Print, Norwich

Contents

Also available in the Church Times Study Guides series:

Jane Williams has taught theology at Trinity College, Bristol, and is presently Visiting Lecturer at King's College London. A regular contributor to the *Church Times*, she is married to Rowan Williams, the Archbishop of Canterbury.

Introduction

Letting Mrs Rochester Out of the Attic

The doctrine of the Trinity was once thought of as the mad wife in the attic. Christians tried, on the whole, never to bring her out into the open, and although she popped out occasionally when no one was looking, for example in the baptism service, or in the prayer of blessing in the 'name of the Father, and of the Son, and of the Holy Spirit', still no one talked about her, and her skeletal traces grew less and less distinct. You can read whole tomes of nineteenth-century theology without ever being confronted with the idea that Christians believe that God is three in one, Trinity, except in the appendices. 'It's not in the Bible, and it doesn't make sense, anyway', was the general opinion.

Nowadays, of course, the Trinity is very popular. It fits very well with our current theological emphases and anxieties to stress that God is social, relational and loving. The Holy Spirit, in particular, who seems to have spent centuries sitting around twiddling his thumbs with nothing much to do, from the human perspective, at least, is now asked to a bewildering variety of parties, wearing all kinds of costumes. Sometimes he, sometimes she, sometimes it; sometimes powerful and dictatorial, issuing messages of ferocious warning and condemnation, sometimes gentle and wholly forgiving; sometimes a monoglot Christian, and sometimes to be found glibly conversing to people of all faiths and none, the Holy Spirit is having a whale of a time.

There are all kinds of reasons for the re-emergence of the Trinity into current theological discourse. One is the greater understanding of and dialogue with Eastern Orthodox Christians, whose way of talking about the Trinity remained much more influenced by their unchanging liturgy and worship than that of Western Christians – so the doctrine of the Trinity has never gone out of fashion in the Orthodox Church. There has also been more and more excavation of the worshipping communities of early Christians, who would have been the first users of the New Testament, and that has helped us to see that the references to 'Father, Son and Holy Spirit' in the New Testament actually take for granted a Christian life embedded in trinitarian worship. In the last fifty years the charismatic movement has brought the Holy Spirit back into the forefront, and encouraged a rethink of the relations in the godhead. And then, of course, we desperately needed a new way of thinking about the Church that would encourage us to remember that the Church is not a building but a community, attempting to make the God it believes in more visible. The focus on God's own trinitarian life suggested that how Christians live together was at least as important a part of mission as the words we used to describe our beliefs.

Charismatic movement – a movement emphasizing 'baptism in the Spirit', and dramatic gifts, like healing, speaking in tongues.

The reams of books written on the doctrine of the Trinity in the last twenty years suggest that this way of describing the nature of God and discovering more about it is something we are hungry for, but that doesn't mean that we don't, in our heart of hearts, sympathize with or forebears who thought it wasn't really in the Bible and it didn't make sense. So let's start with the first of those claims.

1

'It Isn't in the Bible'

The Old Testament

It is perfectly true that the doctrine of the Trinity is not to be found in the Hebrew Scriptures. Although Christians may read references to the 'Spirit of God' (for example, in Ezekiel 37.1 'he brought me out by the spirit of the Lord and set me down in the middle of a valley') as indicating an unrecognized doctrine of the Trinity, scholars of Hebrew say that is actually just a way of saying 'the Lord' in slightly different words. So this is one of the points where we have to be most careful to remember that these are shared Scriptures and read differently by the two religious communities who own them.

But the New Testament is full of references to the Trinity, though without any attempt to explain where this novel way of imagining God came from. It is simply taken for granted. Luke and Acts, John and Paul have the most developed understanding of the Trinity, and there are some New Testament books which have only the most cursory references to the Holy Spirit – the epistle of James doesn't mention it at all, for example. But that is not sufficient reason to believe that it was an optional extra for some of the early church communities. Everything we know about early Christian worship suggests that Father, Son and Holy Spirit were invariably invoked together at the key moments in any worship.

If we look at some of the passages in the New Testament that do have a well-developed theology of the three persons of God, it is obvious that they are talking primarily about Christian experience and assurance, rather than trying to describe how the three persons relate.

The New Testament

Acts

Acts has a number of key descriptions of what we now take for granted about the doctrine of the Trinity. For example:

- The association of the coming of the Holy Spirit with the mission of Jesus, which is to proclaim the kingdom of God

  Acts 1.8 'But you will receive power when the Holy Spirit has come upon you; and you will be my witnesses in Jerusalem, in all Judea and Samaria, and to the ends of the earth.'

- The giving of the Holy Spirit at Pentecost, in tongues of fire, which enables the disciples to speak in many different languages as they proclaim the gospel of Jesus

  Acts 2.1–4 When the day of Pentecost had come, they were all together in one place. And suddenly from heaven there came a sound like the rush of a violent wind, and it filled the entire house where they were sitting. Divided tongues, as of fire, appeared among them, and a tongue rested on each of them. All of them were filled with the Holy Spirit and began to speak in other languages, as the Spirit gave them ability.

- The association of the Holy Spirit with 'power' to perform unusual or difficult feats, from witnessing to Jesus in the face of opposition (cf. Acts 4.8ff. 'Then Peter, filled with the Holy Spirit, said to them, "Rulers of the people and elders..."'), to doing something so wonderful that Simon the Magician offers to pay for the power to do it himself

  Acts 8.14–20 Now when the apostles at Jerusalem heard that Samaria had accepted the word of God, they sent Peter and John to them. The two went down and prayed for them that they might receive the Holy Spirit (for as yet the Spirit had not come upon any of them; they had only been baptized in the name of the Lord Jesus). Then Peter and John laid their hands on them, and they received the Holy Spirit. Now when

Simon saw that the Spirit was given through the laying on of the apostles' hands, he offered them money, saying, 'Give me also this power, so that anyone on whom I lay my hands may receive the Holy Spirit.'

Maddeningly, we do not know how this power was manifested, but it was clearly very obvious.

John's Gospel

Most of what John has to say about the Trinity is found in the chapters that are usually called 'the Farewell Discourses', in John 14–17, although the opening verses of the Gospel are also of vital significance. These are some of the essential elements of John's understanding of the Trinity:

- In the beginning was the Word, and the Word was with God, and the Word was God. He was in the beginning with God. All things came into being through him, and without him not one thing came into being. (John 1.1–3)

This is an unambiguous declaration of the pre-existence of Christ, who always exists with God, and is the creative, outgoing person of the God-head. He is the 'Word', the means by which God is communicated, the means by which it is possible that something should exist outside God himself.

- John, like all the Gospel writers, refers to the visible presence of the Holy Spirit, coming down on Jesus at his baptism. The Holy Spirit confirms who Jesus is and what his ministry is to be.

  And John testified, 'I saw the Spirit descending from heaven like a dove, and it remained on him.' (John 1.32)

Although, typically, John does not directly tell us that this was at Jesus' baptism, he goes on in the next few verses to talk about baptism, and is clearly referring to the event narrated in Matthew 3.16, Mark 1.10 and Luke 3.22. At this point, the Holy Spirit confirms that Jesus is the Son of the Father – a really key New Testament trinitarian moment.

- In chapters 14–17 Jesus is talking to his disciples about what will happen to them after his impending death. The Holy Spirit, the Advocate, is to be key to the disciples' ability to carry on with Jesus' work. He is sent to them by the Father, in the name of Jesus (14.26), to carry on teaching the disciples, and keeping Jesus' own words fresh in their memories.

Paul's Letters

Paul's theology of the Trinity is vivid and varied. His letters are written in the period before the Gospels are written down, and they testify to a strong commitment to understanding God as Trinity very early on in the life of the early Church. Although it would be worthwhile to go through each letter and sift the references to Father, Son and Holy Spirit, again, let's just pick out a few key moments:

- Romans 8 – the whole chapter is full of trinitarian theology – but see

  For all who are led by the Spirit of God are children of God. For you did not receive a spirit of slavery to fall back into fear, but you have received a spirit of adoption. When we cry 'Abba! Father!' it is that very Spirit bearing witness with our spirit that we are children of God, and if children, then heirs, heirs of God and joint heirs with Christ. (Romans 8.14–17)

The Spirit is the one who enables us to stand with the Son and call on the Father. Through the Spirit, we are standing in the place that Christ has made for us, in the life and work of God.

- 1 Corinthians 12–14 shows Paul having an argument with the Corinthian church about 'gifts of the Spirit'. It looks as though this is a church that is quite interested in power and exciting manifestations of the Spirit, but is tempted to take all of this out of the context of what we believe about God. So the letter starts, in chapter 1, talking about 'the foolishness of God', which is 'wiser than human wisdom, and God's weakness is stronger than human strength' (1.25). And this is the context for what Paul goes on to say in chapters 12–14:

Now there are varieties of gifts, but the same Spirit; and there are varieties of services, but the same Lord; and there are varieties of activities, but it is the same God who activates all of them in everyone. (12.4–6)

Notice the deliberately trinitarian structuring of that sentence. Notice, too, that Paul goes on in the rest of this chapter and in the famous chapter 13 on love, and in chapter 14, to work out what it means for us as a community to worship a God who is three in one. It makes our diversity a precious gift, and our unity an absolute imperative.

• So he [Christ] came and proclaimed peace to you who were far off and peace to those who were near; for through him both of us have access in one Spirit to the Father. (Ephesians 2.17)

God's mission to us and through us is trinitarian. Christ comes to bring us close to the Father, and the Spirit guarantees that that is an ongoing, open process, always available. As we preach Christ, we preach him as the path that we can walk, with the Spirit's help and company, leading to the Father.

What can we learn about the Trinity from the Bible?

1 New Testament writers are, on the whole, talking about the experience of God as Trinity in making sense of their faith. They are therefore not very interested in the question of 'God as he is in himself', as opposed to 'God as we experience him' – though the opening of St John's Gospel does assume that the relationship between God and Word predates our existence.

2 But the Trinity is primarily a Jesus-related issue for New Testament Christians. Jesus is the one who opens up the way for us to the Father. The Spirit is the one who keeps Jesus and his work present and active for us now. The work of God, Father, Son and Holy Spirit, has one goal, which is that we should be God's family.

3   God the Trinity is experienced most intensely in two characteristic Christian activities:

- the practice of prayer – praying to the Father, as though we were, like Jesus, his children, because the Holy Spirit helps us to have the confidence to do it.
- The building up of the Christian community, who know themselves to be, like Jesus, God's family, and also know that this is not because of any natural ties or affection but because of the Holy Spirit.

Other kinds of 'gifts of the Spirit' may manifest themselves, but the evidence of the Bible is that they are incidental to these two primary gifts of prayer and body-building.

Exercise

1   Read the whole of Romans 8, and make a list of the things you think it is saying about what the Trinity is and what it does.
2   Think about the way you usually pray. Is your standard way of praying to address the Holy Spirit, Jesus and the Father? Jesus and the Father? Or just God?
3   Have you come across people who talk about the 'gifts of the Spirit'? If so, what do you think they generally mean by that?

2

The God We Meet Is God Himself

One God or three?

We've suggested that when the New Testament writers are talking about the Trinity, they are, generally, speaking about the way in which they and their communities have met God. They are not very interested in answering more abstract questions about how God can be Father, Son and Holy Spirit and yet one God. But inevitably such questions arise, over the centuries, and though we may wish to argue that worship and community are still the places where what we believe about God either makes sense or doesn't, at the same time, we know that any faith that isn't prepared to ask and answer theological questions about itself is probably hiding something.

How many Gods do Christians worship?

One of the interesting and lasting questions that Christians have faced in their understanding of God is are we really 'monotheists', like Jews and Muslims, believing that God is One? Or are we polytheists, like Hindus, only in our case we believe in only three Gods, rather than the Hindu or classical Greek pantheon? The answer is always firmly the former – Christians are monotheists. We believe in only one God, but our God is not a static unity, but a dynamic unity with three centres.

Monotheist – person who believes that there is only one God.

Early Christian theologians thought and talked their way very carefully through this thicket. They did not want to say that God just acts very specially in Jesus, like he acts in the prophets, only more so. They wanted to say that God is actually present, directly, in Jesus. They did not want to say that we continue to experience that Jesus-like presence of God through the Holy Spirit, just as many people have experiences of God through nature, or beauty. They wanted to say that God is still directly present with us, through the Holy Spirit.

But at the same time, they were not satisfied with simply saying that we see different aspects of God at work in Jesus and in the Holy Spirit, but it's really all just the same God. They were convinced that there are genuine differences of function and relationship between Father, Son and Holy Spirit, and that they are not interchangeable. It is never true to say that the Father is the Son or vice versa.

So in all the most carefully crafted statements about God, these two things have to be held in tension – God is One, yet three. Unity and distinction are both characteristic of God.

To begin with, as with the New Testament writers, most early Christian theologians were really only concerned to say that we genuinely experience both the unity of God and the reality of the three persons at work in making and redeeming the world. We know that Father, Son and Holy Spirit are never divided in their purpose – they will one thing, in creating, redeeming and sanctifying. But their roles in this one great purpose are co-operative, rather than simply indistinguishable.

But very quickly, Christians wanted to say more. This is not just the way we happen to experience God. This is the way God really is. We experience God as Father, Son and Holy Spirit, because God *is* Father, Son and Holy Spirit, and always was, even before the creation of the world. He does not become a Father at some point in the dim and distant past, but in his action in creating and redeeming the world, he allows us to see something of his own reality. In fact, it is only because he is this kind of a God, one whose unity is not simple and monochrome, but made up of dynamic interaction, that he creates at all. It is, you might say, a natural thing for such a God to do. Diversity would not be strange and alien and challenging to such a God, it would be fun.

Of course, the minute you go beyond what seems to be common experience, it sounds as though you are saying complicated things that have nothing to do with our faith. It is easy to say 'God was in Christ reconciling the world to himself', and 'the Spirit helps us in our weakness', and to get nods of comprehension from the majority of Christians. But when the language becomes more abstract, and tries to tabulate the raw material of Christian belief and experience, it becomes less compelling. 'Consubstantial, co-eternal, while unending ages run', sounds good while we're singing it, but not when we are trying to explain to a puzzled Muslim why we still believe we are monotheists.

Consubstantial – Latin word, which means the same as the Greek 'homoousios', of the same being or substance.

Co-eternal – all persons of the Trinity are always in existence. None pre-dates the others.

The earliest theologians had exactly the same problem, and came up with all kinds of analogies, to try to help. For example, think of God as the sun, with its light and its heat. One thing, which is experienced in different ways, and cannot make sense without those experiences. A sun with no light or heat is a contradiction in terms. Or think of a human person. Each of us is one, and yet we can think of our minds and emotions separately.

But in case we should start to wonder why we are putting ourselves to all this trouble, it is worth reiterating that two vital things about Christian belief in God are at stake here in the doctrine of the Trinity:

- God is love. It is not just that God occasionally, or even usually, acts lovingly, but that he *is* love. Even without us, Father, Son and Holy Spirit love each other and exist in love. They share that with us, because love is so overflowingly natural to God.
- God really is as we experience him to be. Christian experience of God as Trinity is not just one of several different ways in which God might be experienced. Although it is highly unlikely that we understand very clearly or grasp at all accurately the immensity of God, yet what God shows us about himself is true. In revealing himself through creation, redemption and continuing love as Father, Son and Holy Spirit, God is inviting us into the mysterious reality of his own being.

Unity v. diversity

There has always been a tension, in Christian writing and preaching, between those who want mostly to talk about God, and those who want mostly to talk about Father, Son and Holy Spirit; in other words, between those who emphasize God's unity and those who emphasize his diversity. It will depend on the images and language and worship practices we grow up with, it will depend on our temperament, it will depend on our context and who we are talking to. Traditionally, the great Christian traditions of the East have talked more about God as trinity, whereas the Western ones have tended to talk about the unity of God. In this they were very much influenced by particular theologians who set their mark on a tradition. Let's look at some key influences on both sides.

The Cappadocian Fathers: the relational God

The Cappadocian Fathers are so-called because they lived and worked in Cappadocia, in the Greek-speaking part of the Roman empire in the fourth century. They were Basil, bishop of Caesarea, his brother, Gregory of Nyssa, and Basil's old college friend, Gregory, bishop of Nazianzus. They were famous for all kinds of things. Basil, for example, was one of the founders of Christian monasticism. But they were all heavily involved in the theological controversies of their day, and they came to their discussions about the Trinity fresh from the Arian controversy. Arius, you may remember from *Who Do You Say That I Am?*, taught that Jesus, although much greater and more powerful than any other created being, still was actually one of God's creations, not God himself. Arius' teaching was rejected as heretical, but the controversy he generated helped to formulate the standard Christian creed, so that there would be a brief, clear statement of what must be believed about Jesus. The creed says that Christ is 'of one being [or substance] with God the Father'.

Basil and the two Gregories devoted their considerable theological energies to reinforcing and clarifying this creedal statement about Jesus Christ. So they came to trinitarian theology with their minds already set on how Father and Son could be two and yet 'of one substance'. So when they came up against Christians who did not want to think of the Holy Spirit as God, they simply extrapolated from the work already done on Father and Son. If one substance can exist in two 'beings', then it can exist in three.

> Binitarian – a theology that concentrates only on two persons of the Trinity – generally Father and Son.

The Cappadocians made a number of very helpful technical points:

- 'Father', 'Son' and 'Holy Spirit' are not proper names, like Julie, Jane and Jennifer. They are terms of relation. They are more like 'nephew', 'aunt' and 'sister'. That may be obvious with 'Father and Son', but it applies equally to 'Holy Spirit'. And the fact that 'Holy Spirit' is not a relational term that fits into our human system of relations might help to remind us that our analogies are not very exact. In talking about God, Father, Son and Holy Spirit, we are not talking about three different people, but about a differentiated yet relational being.
- Each member of the Trinity spends its time showing us the others. The Father is known through the Son, the Spirit forms the Son in the Son's followers, the Father gives us the Son, Father and Son together give us the Spirit, Son and Spirit teach us to worship the Father, and so on. There is identity of nature, purpose and will in this God, who is undivided but exists in three Persons. The technical term for talking about this circular way in which God makes himself known is *perichoresis* or *co-inherence*.

> Perichoresis – Greek word, used technically in the discussion of the Trinity to describe how all the persons share equally in the life, actions and goals of the others.

- What the three persons share is 'God-ness', or 'substance' or 'divinity'. What distinguishes them from each other is how they relate to each other. The Father is the one of whom it is inappropriate to ask 'where does he come from' – he simply is. The Son 'comes from' the Father – not in temporal terms, i.e. at some point in time, but in terms of where his substance originates. And the Holy Spirit 'proceeds' from the Father, through the Son. (This is about as clear as mud. Just hang onto the main point, which is that the persons of the Trinity are to be distinguished by how they relate to each other, not because they have different hair colour or characters or likes and dislikes.)

- Although our tiny minds talk in numerical terms, using the words 'three' and 'one', actually these words are not really appropriate to the divine reality. It's just that we haven't got anything better. Very occasionally, like, for example, when we are madly in love, we might get a clue about something that can be more than one and yet united, but most of the time, we are struggling for a proper analogy. But that is what God's being is – a dynamic unity, three yet one. A way of being that our hearts long for, but do not understand.

What the Cappadocians bring out most clearly (though you may be forgiven for thinking that an inappropriate word!) is that all words for God are relational words. We are always trying to make them into proper names, but they are not. They are ways of pointing us constantly to the mysterious, attractive being of God, in whose likeness we are made. We are made with the possibility of being like God in our relatedness to each other and to God, but we keep thinking we are proper names, not terms of relation.

Augustine: the one God

Augustine was a slightly younger contemporary of the Cappadocians, but while they lived and worked in the Greek-speaking part of the Roman empire in the fourth century, Augustine was bishop of Hippo, in North Africa, which was part of the Latin-speaking Roman empire. Augustine says that he didn't speak much Greek, and we just don't know whether or not he had read the work of any of the Cappadocians.

Like them, Augustine was clear that the terms 'Father, Son and Holy Spirit' are relational terms, that all the persons of the Trinity are united in will and action, and that what distinguishes them is how they relate to each other.

But three things in Augustine's theology did lead him to put more emphasis on the one-ness of God than his three-ness.

1   Augustine is talking to a world which thinks it knows what 'divine nature' is. Few people in Augustine's day were what we would call atheists. So Augustine is trying to show that this divinity is what Christians call 'God', and that it can best be described as Trinity. In other words, where the Cappadocians might start from God the Father, Augustine is more likely to start with 'God', and move from there to Father, Son and Holy Spirit.

2   Augustine is much more concerned to work out some coherent things to say about the Holy Spirit than the Cappadocians were. So, for example, he asks himself why we don't say that the Father has two sons, as opposed to a Son and a Holy Spirit. His answer, which he doesn't just make up, but tries to derive from the Bible, is that the Holy Spirit comes from both Father and Son. The Spirit is the love which unites Father and Son, it is the gift produced by their communion.

3   Augustine believed that, since we are made in the image of God, there will be vestiges of the trinitarian image in us, though horribly obscured and muddied by sin. He used a great many analogies of threefold processes that we regularly take for granted, to try to give his readers some ideas of how something can be both three and one. He talked about the human mind, its knowledge of itself and its self-love. Or memory, understanding and will, as three movements of the same mind. Augustine wrote, speaking to God, 'You have made us for yourself, and our hearts are restless till they find their rest in you.' It is as though, deep inside us, we know that we are made to a pattern, but we cannot see it. We are made in the image of God, Father, Son and Holy Spirit, and cannot rest until we find that way of being.

Because Augustine's way of speaking about the Spirit is quite abstract, and because the analogies he uses are drawn from individual experience, he is often thought to have contributed to the decline of genuine trinitarian theology in the West. It is true that most theologians and Christians have focused on the relationship between the Father and the Son, because that is something we think we can begin to understand. It is also true that Christian art very often cannot find an appropriate image of the Holy Spirit, who is often seen as a tiny dove, where Father and Son are given human faces. But Augustine's great contribution is to remind us that this is the image, the life, the way of being that draws us, this mysterious yet compelling life of God in Trinity. And if the Holy Spirit is more anonymous to us than Father and Son, maybe that is because the role he fulfils, if Augustine is right, is the one that we find hardest. He is the gift of love that draws us together, uniting us into one, making us interdependent and unified, like Father, Son and Holy Spirit.

Augustine, like Basil, Gregory and Gregory, was a Christian leader first and foremost. His theology is done in this context of responsibility for a Christian community, often under pressure both internally and externally. Augustine's last writing is done as the Roman empire in the West crumbles. Civilization as he and all his contemporaries knew it was under threat as Augustine wrote *The City of God*. It is no abstract matter to him, but a question of hope or despair, whether our own human life is rooted in this world or in the life of the eternal God. And if some of what these early theologians wrote about the Trinity sounds to us abstract, perhaps it is important to remember that Augustine shared his home and his worship day by day with fellow Christians. He is talking about something that he, like us, is trying to live out. That is why it is so essential to emphasize that the God we meet in our unmerited salvation is the God we shall meet again, Father, Son and Holy Spirit, in eternity.

How tidying up theology can lead to division; or the vexed case of the filioque clause

Augustine probably did imply that the Spirit is given by the Father *and* the Son, and his description of the Holy Spirit as 'the bond of love' does tend to make the Holy Spirit seem less personal than the Father and the Son. The influence of his theology was part of what led to the great split between the Eastern and the Western Christian churches over what is called the *filioque* clause. 'Filioque' is the Latin for 'and the Son', and it is said in all Western creeds when we talk about the Holy Spirit. We say that 'he proceeds from the Father and the Son', whereas Eastern creeds do not. Eastern Christians think it more accurately reflects both the Bible and a proper philosophical theology to say that the Spirit proceeds from the Father alone, though most would be happy to say 'with the Son' or 'through the Son'. Like all major Christian controversies, this one, which led to the division of the Christian Church, was not just about theology. It was also about power-relations. The Western Church decided, unilaterally, to insert their own interpretation of the procession of the Holy Spirit into the creeds, and seemed to assume that all the rest of the Church must follow. Not unnaturally, the ancient churches of the East did not see it that way.

> Filioque – Latin word, meaning 'and the Son'.
>
> Procession of the Holy Spirit – technical term to describe how the Holy Spirit comes from the Father. He is not 'begotten', like the Son, but 'proceeds'.

It may seem extraordinary to us that such a thing can have been allowed to split the Church. And it is tragically true that once you break something apart, it is much harder to put together again. Eastern and Western Churches now have centuries of different development and separate hierarchy to try to overcome, which will not be wiped out, even if we could agree a formula of words for the creed.

Losing sight of the Trinity / Putting Mrs Rochester away

Of course, the fourth century does not mark the end of thinking and praying about the doctrine of the Trinity. But the puzzle is to understand why, in so much popular piety before the coming of the charismatic movement, this way of understanding the nature of God should have become more or less an optional extra. For Augustine and the Cappadocians, it is the key to God. It makes God's nature both like and yet unlike ours, it makes God's being that for which we long, to which we aspire, but which we know we can only share in because God himself draws us in.

Perhaps we could point to the growth of individualism, which makes us uneasy about saying that we are incomplete unless part of a bigger unity. Perhaps the Romantic movement, with its intense interest in feelings and emotions, encouraged the willingness to focus more and more on what goes on between Father and Son which is, in any case, easier for our imaginations than it is to try to picture the trinity-in-unity. Perhaps the growth of literary and historical criticism, which brought the craze for trying to find the 'historical' Jesus, deflected attention from Father and Spirit.

People argue fiercely about whether or not the charismatic movement in the twentieth century has led to renewal, but whatever else it has or hasn't done, it has definitely contributed to the rediscovery of the doctrine of the Trinity. Much early charismatic worship was rather light in content, and there was a tendency to get fixated on the dramatic and exciting manifestations of the Spirit, rather than the ones that Paul thinks are actually characteristic of the Spirit – 'love, joy, peace, patience, kindness, generosity, faithfulness, gentleness and self-control' (Galatians 5.22–3). Initially, too, the movement was very suspicious of theology, which it considered to be a dry intellectualism. Worship, it believed, is the proper place of Christian formation. But the deepening theology of the movement and its increasing commitment to mainstream church life embedded and encouraged a renewed longing for a fully trinitarian theology of God. If it also encouraged the rebirth of the practising theologian, one who saw Christian faith, life and worship as interconnected, and did not think of commitment as compromising academic integrity, perhaps that, too, is no bad thing.

The growth of ecumenism, too, brought Western Christians into a more profound contact with the theology of Eastern Christians, whose liturgy and practices have been far less influenced by Reformation and Modernity than ours, and who retain a way of talking about Father, Son and Holy Spirit that would sound familiar to the Cappadocians. Iconography, like the famous Rublev icon of the Trinity, and the spirituality of, for example, the Jesus Prayer, are now deep in the bloodstream of the whole Christian Church.

Exercise

1 Find out all you can about your nearest Orthodox church. If possible, arrange to join them for a service.
2 Look at the readings and prayers set in the Anglican lectionary for Trinity Sunday and for Pentecost. Use them as a basis to put together the vital things you might want to say about God the Holy Trinity.

For Pentecost, the primary New Testament reading is Acts 2.1–21, but the lectionary also suggests 1 Corinthians 12.3b–13; Romans 8.22–7; Romans 8.14–17; John 20.19–23; John 15.26–7; 16.4b–15; John 14.8–27.

The collect for Pentecost is:

God, who at this time taught the hearts of your faithful people by sending to them the light of your Holy Spirit, grant us by the same Spirit to have a right judgement in all things and evermore to rejoice in his holy comfort, through the merits of Christ Jesus our Saviour, who is alive and reigns with you, in the unity of the Holy Spirit, one God, now and for ever.

For Trinity Sunday, the lectionary suggests 2 Corinthians 13.11–13; Romans 8.12–17; Romans 5.1–5; Matthew 28.16–20; John 3.1–17; John 16.12–15.

The collect for Trinity Sunday is:

Almighty and everlasting God, you have given us your servants grace, by the confession of a true faith, to acknowledge the glory of the eternal Trinity and in the power of the divine majesty to worship the Unity, keep us steadfast in this faith, that we may evermore be defended from all adversities; through Jesus Christ your Son our Lord, who is alive and reigns with you, in the unity of the Holy Spirit, one God, now and forever.

3   Find a copy of Rublev's icon of the Trinity and use it as a focus for your prayer. Notice the similarities between the three figures, but also their slight differences, in position, in what they are wearing and what colour their clothes are. If green represents new life, and brown represents earthliness, which figure do you think is which? Notice that the figures are androgynous. Notice that the side of the table nearest to the viewer is empty – that is a space at God's table for us. (There are good resources for using Rublev's icon on the web.)

3

The Fellowship of the Three

Understanding the Trinity Today

Christians know, in their heart of hearts, that the doctrine of the Trinity has something to say about how they should live together. We know that that is our weakest point. Best not to think too much about it. But if we really believe that this is the God in whose image we are made, and that our ultimate goal is to participate in this divine life, then it cannot be optional to our life together now.

Some parts of our Christian lives seem more naturally to lend themselves to experiencing the Trinity. For example, there are times, however few and far between, when our personal prayer does suddenly seem to be taken over by the Holy Spirit praying in us and, just for a moment, we can become aware that we are joining in the conversation that happens constantly all around us, the conversation between Father, Son and Holy Spirit. Most of the time, we cannot hear it or feel it, but it is there.

Or at the eucharistic table, we can make a conscious decision to remember all those Christians throughout the world who are sharing bread and wine at that moment. As we gather at one time, in one place, we can be aware of the great company of heaven and earth, made one, whether we know it or not, like it or not, by participating in the body and blood of Christ, becoming the body of Christ. That is not our doing or our choice. It is what God has done.

Sometimes holy people can make us experience what it would be like to live the life of the Trinity. The twentieth-century Russian theologian Vladimir Lossky suggested that the anonymity of the Holy Spirit is meant to make us look for his work in each other. The Spirit takes his 'incarnation' in the lives of Christian saints, who draw us into the love and life of God, and in whom we can glimpse the face of Christ, praying to the Father for us. We talk about being 'inspired', and that is a very good word to describe what is happening. We are breathing in the Holy Spirit, through the life and witness of those who know him and breathe him better than we do. For us, breathing in the life of the Holy Spirit can be like trying to swim under water. We can only do it for a very short time. Saints are people who have been practising for years, and they can not only teach us a few tricks, but help us to believe that this could be our natural medium.

But if it is easy to identify the life of God the Trinity in moments when we are moved or filled with joy, the cross challenges us to find this life in other ways, too. It challenges us to find the overflowing, never-ending life of God in suffering, such as Jesus endured, and even in death. Because Jesus has been there, so has the life of God, and it is still there for us, even though we cannot always see it or feel it. Nothing can separate us from the love of God in Christ Jesus, Paul says. The Holy Spirit, the life-giver, is present even in death, still praying in us, still joining us to the life of God. Christians are resurrection people, not out of mindless optimism, but because in the cross, God, Father, Son and Holy Spirit, demonstrate the invincible strength of their loving life, and their unshakeable willingness to share it with us.

For God to make it possible for us, in our alienation, separation and sin, to share in his life again, cost the cross. We can only talk about it in ways that are at least largely metaphorical and wholly shocking, but it is as though God is prepared to have the eternal unity of his life torn apart on the cross to make room for us. Unimaginably, the only-begotten Son, who is of God's own being, says, 'My God, my God, why have you forsaken me?' If Augustine is right to call the Holy Spirit 'the bond of love', then that bond is stretched to breaking point on the cross. But it holds. It holds because it is the life of God, and now we know that what God will do to share his life with us is without limit.

And that must mean, surely, that we do not experience the trinitarian life of God only in moments of peace or joy, but also in moments when our fellowship is stretched to the limits, and when we are challenged to discover how far we are prepared to let our life be pulled apart to make room for others. The temptation is always to cut the ties because the pain of holding on to each other is too great, the confusion and unclarity too damaging. But if God had taken that route with us, where would we be now? Perhaps this is the most sombre challenge of our trinitarian God: are we prepared to believe in the reality of this life of unity only through diversity? Are we prepared to sacrifice something of our own autonomy for this vision? Are we prepared to follow our God and never believe that separation and death are stronger than unity and life? If we Christians could really believe in our three-personed God, and live as though we did, we could begin to demonstrate this life to the world, a life richer, more exciting and more fundamental to the world than anything we can possibly imagine by ourselves.

So perhaps the most revealing trinitarian prayer is that one that we use so often that we hardly need even to think about the words any more. 'The grace of our Lord, Jesus Christ, and the love of God, and the fellowship of the Holy Spirit, be with us all, evermore.' So much is encapsulated in those words. God's love reaches out for us, freely, beyond anything we can deserve or expect, in the life and death of Jesus Christ, and then the Holy Spirit, the gift of binding, unending love, holds us together, in gratitude and mission.

Exercise

1 Have you met people who made you feel that the Holy Spirit might be 'incarnate' in them?
2 How well does the life of the Christian group you know best convey a sense of excitement about unity through diversity?
3 Are there issues over which Christian churches should properly divide now? If so, what are they? If not, why not?

4

Encountering the Trinity

Two Exercises

Prayer

'Why do we pray? God already knows everything, so isn't it presumptuous to think we could somehow "get" God to do something? Is prayer just between us and God, with us as pitiful creatures abject before the Almighty, hoping to wring some little concession from the divine mercy? Certainly, we have more than a few clues that this is a false picture indeed. Jesus taught the disciples that the first words to say in prayer are "Our Father", so our prayer must be something we do in fellowship with Jesus, namely talking with his Father and ours. In turn, that means we are talking not to an anonymous and inscrutable deity but to someone Jesus knows intimately and whom we are being invited to know in him. We have Paul's numerous references to the role of the Holy Spirit in our prayer, particularly in his letter to the Romans. "For we do not know how to pray as we ought, but that very Spirit intercedes with sighs too deep for words" (Romans 8.26). Paul suggests that we better give up the idea that we are the ones praying at all . . . If God is God because of the loving communion of the Trinity, then when we pray we are invited more deeply into this exchange of love. Prayer is really God happening in us, you could say, or – more accurately – our coming into fuller being as we pray in the divine communion. So when we ask for things in prayer, we are not trying to coax God into doing something God had never thought of until we happened along with the bright idea. Instead, God is trying to renew our minds and hearts in the likeness of the divine yearning' (Mark McIntosh, 2000, *Mysteries of Faith*, Cowley Press, pp. 45–7).

Exercise

1 Do you find this description of prayer illuminating? Does it leave anything out? How does it match with your own experience of prayer?

2 Find a prayer book that is regularly used in your church, and look at some of the prayers in it. How central is the doctrine of the Trinity in those prayers? (If yours is not a church with a tradition of set liturgy, listen carefully to the prayers at the next service you go to, and reflect on the trinitarian content.)

3 This is the Anglican collect for the Third Sunday after Trinity:

> Almighty God, you have broken the tyranny of sin and have sent the Spirit of your Son into our hearts whereby we call you Father; give us grace to dedicate our freedom to your service, that we and all creation may be brought to the glorious liberty of the children of God; through Jesus Christ your Son our Lord, who is alive and reigns with you, in the unity of the Holy Spirit, one God, now and forever.

Compare this prayer with Romans 8. Is it a good interpretation of the passage? Pray the prayer.

God is Love

In *The Crucified God* Moltmann is particularly concerned to show how Jesus' death on the cross brings into contact with God those who would previously have assumed they were beyond the love of God. Because Jesus dies as one condemned by those who should speak for God, as one apparently abandoned by his God, as one condemned as a criminal by the legal authorities, the Holy Spirit is now able to bring all who are rejected and godforsaken into the life of God. This is powerful polemical writing, but where does it leave the life and witness of the Church?

> God does not just love as he is angry, chooses or rejects. He *is* love, that is, he exists in love. He exists as love in the event of the cross. Thus in the concepts of earlier systematic theology it is possible to talk of a *homoousion*, in respect of an identity of substance, the community of

will of the Father and the Son on the cross. However, the unity contains not only identity of substance but also the wholly and utterly different character and inequality of the event on the cross. In the cross, Father and Son are most deeply separated in forsakenness and at the same time are most inwardly one in their surrender. What proceeds from this event between Father and Son is the Spirit which justifies the godless, fills the forsaken with love and even brings the dead alive, since even the fact that they are dead cannot exclude them from this event of the cross; the death in God also includes them. (J. Moltmann, *The Crucified God*, p. 244)

Homoousios – Greek word, meaning 'of one being or substance'.

1 Earlier in this extraordinary book, Moltmann argues that the Son suffers on the cross, feeling abandoned by the Father, and that the Father suffers the death of his Son. This event breaks open the life of God, to make room for us, and the Holy Spirit draws God and us back together. How do you respond to this picture? Can you find biblical backing for it? What does it leave out, or include?

2 As with many powerful statements about the cross, the emotional focus is on what is going on between Father and Son. Why do you think Moltmann uses the words he does to describe the role of the Spirit in the cross?

Singing the Trinity

Exercise

Look at the hymnbook or songbook you are most familiar with, and do a rough count of the number of songs you think contain significant references to the Trinity.

Here is one:

Filled with the Spirit's power, with one accord
the infant Church confessed its risen Lord.
O Holy Spirit, in the Church today
No less your power of fellowship display.

Now with the mind of Christ set us on fire,
That unity may be our great desire.
Give joy and peace; give faith to hear your call,
And readiness in each to work for all.

Widen our love, good Spirit, to embrace
In your strong care the men of every race.
Like wind and fire with life among us move,
Till we are known as Christ's and Christians prove.
(J. R. Peacey)

1 Do you like this hymn?
2 Identify other good trinitarian hymns.
3 This one is addressed to the Spirit. How often have you heard prayers and hymns to the Spirit?

Each of these writers has a burning core of longing at the heart of what they say about the Trinity. McIntosh is trying to convey the extraordinary idea that, through prayer, we are allowing God to 'happen in us', and that where God happens, there is life and hope and renewal.

Moltmann is taking that key insight and looking around at the world, full of death and despair and decay, and saying, 'This is not the last word.' Because God the Holy Trinity breaks open his life for us on the cross, God's own eternal, unending love is seen as the reality of the world. God, Father, Son and Holy Spirit, are love so intense that they can never be separated, and that is what we are promised, too. We are promised life, lived fully in the love of God, because God has chosen to make room for us.

Peacey and Moltmann both agree that if our God really is Trinity, then we have to believe that we are called to find our own life only in our common fellowship. God chooses not to live in his own self-sufficient love, and we have to make the same choice, too. We have to learn better ways of living together as Christians and sharing the life-giving love of God with the rest of the world.

Exploring the Trinity puts demanding, joyful, self-sacrificial love at the heart of the Christian understanding of God and the Christian calling to follow Christ. 'Love' is not a soft concept, but a hard and thrilling way of living, that refuses any definition that is going to leave other people out of our life, our calling, our mission.

Further Reading and Resources

Books

British Council of Churches, 1989, *The Forgotten Trinity*, London: Church House Publishing

Christopher Cocksworth, 1997, *Holy, Holy, Holy: Worshipping the Trinitarian God*, London: Darton, Longman & Todd

Doctrine Commission of the Church of England, 1989, *We Believe in the Holy Spirit*, London: Church House Publishing

Paul Fiddes, 2000, *Participating in God: A Pastoral Doctrine of the Trinity*, London: Darton, Longman & Todd

Catherine LaCugna, 2000, *God for Us: The Trinity and Christian Life*, San Francisco: HarperSanFrancisco

Jürgen Moltmann, 1973, *The Crucified God*, Eng. trans., 2nd edn, London: SCM Press

Jürgen Moltmann, 1980, *The Trinity and the Kingdom of God*, Eng. trans., London: SCM Press

Tom Smail, 1994, *The Giving Gift: The Holy Spirit in Person*, London: Darton, Longman & Todd

John V. Taylor, 1972, *Go-Between God*, London: SCM Press

Thomas F. Torrance, 1996, *The Christian Doctrine of God: One Being in Three Persons*, Edinburgh: T&T Clark

Thomas G. Weinandy, 1995, *The Father's Gift of Sonship*, Edinburgh: T&T Clark

Hymn books and prayer books

Look particularly at sections on the Trinity, but also at whether references to the Trinity seem to be found only in these sections, or whether they are more pervasive.

The web

Try typing in 'charismatic movement', and you will get quite a lot of interesting material, both historical, wacky and current.

You could also contact organizations like Soul Survivor and New Wine, which have strong charismatic loyalties, and a desire to train and equip young Christian leaders.